OXFORD TO
MORETON-IN-MARSH

Vic Mitchell and Keith Smith

 Middleton Press

Cover picture: Seen at Kingham with the 2.0pm from Hereford to Oxford on 3rd October 1953 is no. 4938 Liddington Hall. *"On shed" is 0-6-0 no. 3204. The bridge once carried through trains between Swansea and Newcastle. (N.W.Sprinks)*

> **Published to commemorate 150 years of the Oxford to Evesham line, which opened in 1853.**

First published September 2003

ISBN 1 904474 15 2

.

© *Middleton Press, 2003*

Design   David Pede
Typesetting   Barbara Mitchell

Published by
          Middleton Press
          Easebourne Lane
          Midhurst, West Sussex
          GU29 9AZ
Tel: 01730 813169
Fax: 01730 812601
Email: info@middletonpress.co.uk
www.middletonpress.co.uk

Printed & bound by Biddles Ltd, Kings Lynn

INDEX

ACKNOWLEDGEMENTS

We are very grateful for the assistance received from many of those mentioned in the credits also to A.E.Bennett, W.R.Burton, R.S Carpenter, L.Crosier, G.Croughton, G.Heathcliffe, N.Langridge, B.W Leslie, S.C Nash, Mr D. and Dr S.Salter, E.Youldon and particularly our ever supportive wives, Barbara Mitchell and Janet Smith.

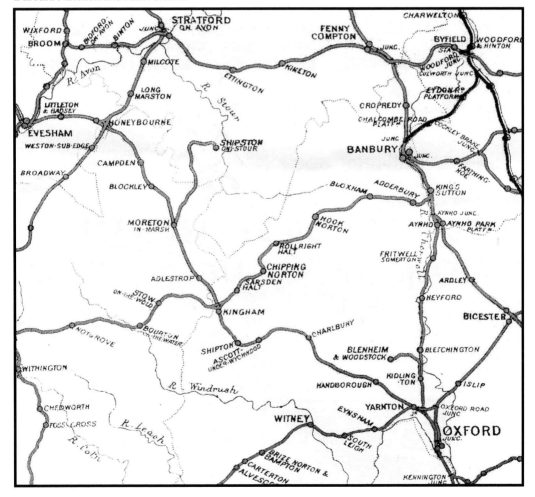

I.   Railway Clearing House map of 1947. The intermediate branch stations had closed by that time, but are shown on map XVI near picture 107.

GEOGRAPHICAL SETTING

The River Evenlode flows into the Thames west of Oxford, having risen near Moreton-in-Marsh. The railway runs close to its 30-mile meandering course, crossing it twelve times.

The line is on Oxford Clay for its first six miles or so and then passes over Oolitic Limestone in a narrow valley in the vicinity of Charlbury. It continues over Lower Lias Limestone for the remainder of the route, rising gently.

Most of the journey is in Oxfordshire, the Gloucestershire boundary being north of Kingham. The impressive landscapes of the area form part of the northern section of the Cotswold Hills, the route thus having the marketing name of the "Cotswold Line".

The maps are to the scale of 25 ins to 1 mile, with north at the top, unless otherwise indicated.

Shipston-on-Stour Branch

The route was almost entirely on Lower Lias Limestone and began on the fairly level land surrounding Moreton-in-Marsh, where the infant River Evenlode occupies only a few ditches.

The line soon dropped down off the watershed into the valley of Knee Brook, which is a tributary of the north flowing River Stour. The route took to high ground again illogically, owing to its history, before descending to the small trading centre of Shipston-on-Stour. The line would have taken a more direct route had it not utilised as much of the earlier tramway as possible.

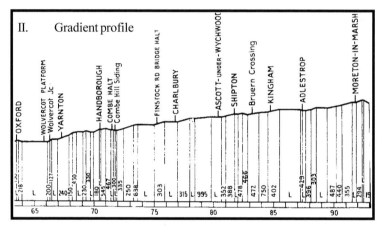

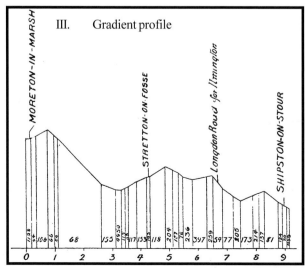

HISTORICAL BACKGROUND

The first railway in Oxford was a branch from the Great Western Railway at Didcot and it opened to a terminus southeast of the present station in 1844. It was extended north to Banbury in 1852 and was of broad gauge (7ft 0¼ ins).

The London & North Western Railway built a standard gauge line from Bletchley to its own terminus in Oxford and opened it in 1851.

The Oxford, Worcester & Wolverhampton Railway received its Act on 4th August 1845. The section between Oxford and Evesham came into use on 4th June 1853 and was mixed gauge, but no regular broad gauge service was operated. The OWWR became part of the West Midland Railway in 1860, which in turn was absorbed by the GWR in 1863. The broad gauge rails were not usable after 1st April 1869.

Branches from the route followed thus: to Shipston-on-Stour (1853-58 and 1889-1929), to Chipping Norton (1855-1962), to Bourton-on-the-Water (1862-1962) and to Fairford (1873-1962). The dates stated are for passenger services. The middle two became part of the Banbury-Cheltenham route in 1887.

The line became part of the Western Region of British Railways on 1st January 1948 upon nationalisation and was singled between Wolvercot Junction and Ascott-under-Wychwood on 29th November 1971.

Privatisation resulted in Thames Trains Ltd. operating most services from 13th October 1996. The 7½ year franchise soon came under the control of the Go-Ahead Group plc.

Shipston-on-Stour Branch

The 16-mile long Stratford & Moreton Tramway was authorised in 1821 and opened on 5th September 1826. It was the only railway to have been built by the famous road engineer, Thomas Telford and was part of an ambitious scheme to link the waterways of the Midlands and the North with those of the South, near Oxford, but lack of funds prevented completion. However, a 2¾ mile branch to Shipston-on-Stour was opened on 11th February 1836.

The OWWR took over the enterprise in 1847 and instituted a passenger service between Moreton and Stratford-upon-Avon from 1st August 1853. The coaches were horse-drawn, as the track comprised short fish bellied rails resting on stone blocks. The line reverted to freight only on 30th September 1858, but Stratford received conventional trains on the OWWR branch from Honeybourne on 11th July 1859.

The tramway was eventually relaid as a railway and opened to all traffic between Moreton and Shipston on 1st July 1889, the remainder being abandoned in around 1900 and lifted in 1917.

Passenger service between Moreton and Shipston was withdrawn on 8th July 1929, but freight continued until 2nd May 1960.

PASSENGER SERVICES

Down trains running on at least five days each week are considered in this section.

Initially there were five weekday trains between Oxford and Dudley, all standard gauge; two were termed expresses. There were two trains on Sundays, calling at all stations.

The first OWWR trains from Oxford comprised only a few coaches of its own, most of the train having been formed of LNWR stock running from Euston via Bletchley. The two sections were joined at Handborough. This arrangement lasted until September 1861.

By 1869, there were two stopping trains, two semi-fasts and one express on weekdays and on Sundays there were just two slow trains. Twenty years later, the service was similar, but there was just one extra weekday train, an evening express.

The number of trains stopping at the stations at both ends of the route are shown overleaf:

	Weekdays	Sundays	
1909	8	2	(a)
1933	9	2	(b)
1949	9	4	(c)
1969	8	3	(d)
1989	11	6	(e)
2003	15	12	(f)

(a) There was also a 2.25pm from Oxford to Kingham which connected there with a Cheltenham to Worcester Express.

(b) Included three trains from London with dining cars.

(c) As (b) with two such trains on Sundays as well.

(d) As (c) with two of the weekday trains with buffets.

(e) On Sundays, one train ran to Manchester and another to Edinburgh and Glasgow.

(f) One service daily was provided by First Great Western.

June 1860

July 1933

TIME TABLE OF THROUGH SERVICE BETWEEN EUSTON AND THE OXFORD, WORCESTER & WOLVERHAMPTON RAILWAY, JUNE, 1860.

Through coaches between Euston and the O.W. & W.R. by all trains.

LONDON, OXFORD, KINGHAM, EVESHAM, and WORCESTER.

Shipston-on-Stour Branch

Timetables from 1853 to 1858 showed departures (behind a horse) from Stratford-upon-Avon at 6.15am and 4.15pm with the return being at 9.45am and 6.20pm from Moreton. Probably formed of a single small coach, the service reversed at Shipston-on-Stour and Darlingscott Junction.

From the reopening in 1889 until 1915, there were generally four trains on weekdays. The figure was reduced to two for exactly two years (1917-18), due to wartime restrictions. Subsequently, and until closure, there were three.

There is no evidence of any Sunday services. The GWR did offer its own replacement bus service, although for only about three months.

February 1890

```
SHIPSTON-ON-STOUR BRANCH.
          Great Western.

Paddington Sta.,            gov mrn aft gov
LONDON 20........dep 5 30 1010 1 15 4 45
Moreton-in-the-Marsh. 9a8 1  5 5 10 8 20
Longdon Road * ........ 9 38 1 35 5 40 8 50
Shipston-on-Stour..arr 9 53 1 50 5 55 9  5
           Up.              gov mrn aft gov
Shipston-on-Stour..dep 7  5 1135 3 30 7 15
Longdon Road *..f 7 9,28 7 20 1150 3 45 7 30
Moreton-in-the-Marsh .7 50 1220 4 15 8  0
LONDON (Pad) 23 . arr 1025 3 30 7 20 11 0
a Leaves at 9 35 mrn. on Shipston Stock
  Sale Days. * Station for Ilmington.
```

August 1915

	MORETON-IN-MARSH and SHIPSTON-ON-STOUR.—Great Western.							
Miles	Down.	Week Days only.			Miles	Up.	Week Days only.	
		mrn	aft	aft			mrn	aft
	Moreton-in-Marsh dep.	9 22	1 15	5 5		Shipston-on-Stour......dep.	6 30	1155 3 25
4½	Stretton-on-Fosse	9 42	1 31	5 25	2½	Longdon Road *	6 41	1210 3 40
6½	Longdon Road*	9 52	1 41	5 35	4½	Stretton-on-Fosse	6 51	1220 3 50
9	Shipston-on-Stour arr.	10 7	1 52	5 50	9	Moreton-in-Marsh 92 ... arr.	7 7	1240 4 10

* Station for Ilmington (1½ miles).

July 1917

	MORETON-IN-MARSH and SHIPSTON-ON-STOUR.—Great Western.						
Miles	Down.	Week Days only.		Miles	Up.	Week Days only.	
		mrn	aft			mrn	aft
	Moreton-in-Marsh dep.	9 25	5 0		Shipston-on-Stour......dep.	1130	6 10
4½	Stretton-on-Fosse			2½	Longdon Road ‖	1145	6 25
6½	Longdon Road ‖	9 59	5 25	4½	Stretton-on-Fosse		
9	Shipston-on-Stour arr.	10 8	5 40	9	Moreton-in-Marsh 92 .. arr.	1210	6 50

Station for Ilmington (1½ miles).

August 1928

	MORETON-IN-MARSH and SHIPSTON-ON-STOUR.						
Miles	Down.	Wk. Dys. only.		Miles	Up.	Wk. Dys. only.	
		mrn	aft			mrn	aft
	Moreton-in-Marsh dep.	10 5	5 0		Shipston-on-Stour ......dep.	1145	6 5
4	Stretton-on-Fosse	1025	5 20	2½	Longdon Road D	12 0	6 16
6½	Longdon Road D	1035	5 30	5	Stretton-on-Fosse	1210	6 26
9	Shipston-on-Stour arr.	1046	5 41	9	Moreton-in-Marsh 114 .. arr.	1230	6 50

D Station for Ilmington (1½ miles).

July 1929

	MORETON-IN-MARSH and ILMINGTON (Road Motor Service).								
Miles	Down.	Week Days only.			Miles	Up.	Week Days only.		
		mrn	aft	aft	aft			mrn	mrn	non	aft	aft
	Moreton-in-Marsh dep.	10 0	1 10	6 55		Ilmington ....dep.	11 5	5 45 7 S50
—	Stretton-on-Fosse Turn.	1015	1 25	7 10		Shipston-on-Stour	9 15	1122 12 0	6 10 8 S 5
—	Shipston-on-Stour	1030	1 40 5 20	7 25		Stretton-on-Fosse Turn ...	9 30	1215	6 25
—	Ilmington ....arr.	1052		5 37 7S47		Moreton-in-Marsh 114.. arr.	9 45	1230	6 40

§ Saturdays only.

OXFORD

IV.   The 1921 survey at 6ins to 1 mile has the GWR line from Didcot at the bottom. It runs over Botley Road into the 1852 station, to the east of which is the 1851 terminus of the LNWR. Named "Rewley Road", it was in use for passengers until 1951 and for goods until 1984. Port Meadow Halt is shown near the top of the map - this was on the LNWR route. The original GWR terminus was south of the city centre.

1.   The 1852 station had a roof over the through lines until 1890, when it was rebuilt to the form seen. The timber structures were replaced by more wooden buildings in 1910-11. (Lens of Sutton)

2.   Approaching the up platform in 1904 is 2-2-2 no. 158. The connection on the right ran to a two-road carriage shed until the platform was lengthened almost to the bridge, near the sign for SUTTONS. (P.Q.Treloar coll.)

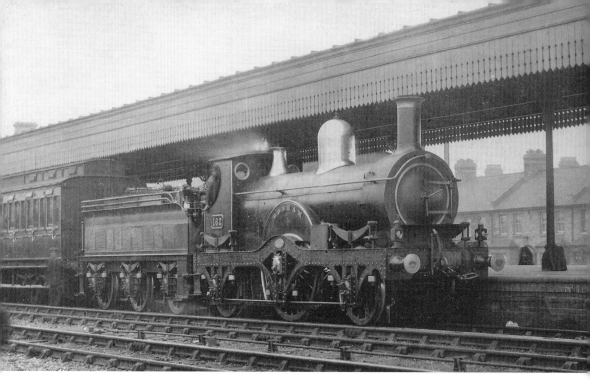

3.　　The 1910 canopy on the down platform is evident in this fine record of 2-2-2 no. 162 *Cobham*. The down bay on the far side of the platform was commonly used by trains for Fairford and Blenheim & Woodstock. (P.Q.Treloar coll.)

4.　　No. 9654 is seen from the end of the up platform bringing empty stock for a Fairford service into the bay. The perforated signal was for reversing movements. On the right is the ex-LNWR swing bridge and partially obscured by the first coach is Station North Box. (N.W.Sprinks)

5. Station North Box had a 100-lever frame and was called "Engine Shed Signal Box" when photographed in 1929. The name was changed in 1942 and closure took place on 29th October 1973. A panel was installed in a cabin near the down platform. (Brunel University/Mowat coll.)

6. The down side building was similar to that on the up side, but it had only one chimney stack. A Standard Eight and a Standard Vanguard flank the booking office entrance in this view from around 1960. (D.Lawrence)

7.   Station North Box is almost hidden by no. 5932 *Haydon Hall* as it runs on the up through line in about 1958. The engine shed is also included in this fine panorama of GWR signals. Much freight passes through and in February 2003 there were usually ten container trains daily. (P.Q.Treloar)

8.   This was the quaint welcome to passengers from the west. The garden shed was occupied by the Oxford & District Society of Model and Experimental Engineers and was flanked by posters offering alternative routes to ill health. (J.Parker)

OXFORD STATION

TO TRAINS FOR
BIRMINGHAM WORCESTER
FAIRFORD & THE NORTH
& L.M.R. TRAINS FOR
BLETCHLEY & CAMBRIDGE

TO TRAINS FOR
LONDON READING SWINDON
THE SOUTH COAST
THE WEST OF ENGLAND
& SOUTH WALES

9. The simple shed-like accommodation provided by the GWR was extensively decayed and was demolished in 1971. An Intercity DMU stands at the up platform on 7th July 1971, while an up through train is signalled. This temporary footbridge was provided during the closure of the subway. (H.C.Casserley)

10. BR chose to erect an even simpler building using its CLASP system, which was similar to the emergency housing provided in wartime. Totally unsuited to a city noted for its quality of architecture, it fortunately rotted quicker than its predecessor. (D.Thompson)

→

11. An example of the second generation of DMUs is berthed at the former parcels platform, while no. 150131 represents the third and is in the up bay on 30th January 1993. It will form the 20.40 to Worcester and Great Malvern and is in Centro livery. Examples of the first generation appear in picture 17, and the other side of the 1910 canopy is on the left of the next view. (M.J.Stretton)

→

12. A new building was completed in the Spring of 1990 and a fully glazed footbridge replaced the gloomy tunnel. No. 166219 represented the latest style of DMU when photographed running from Hereford to Paddington on 6th March 1999. (M.Turvey)

Other views of this station can be found in *Branch Line to Fairford, Branch Lines to Princes Risborough* and *Didcot to Banbury*.

13.	The new station was spacious and airy, its styling adding greatly to the area. A bus station was created in the forecourt and an extensive cycle park was provided to the south of the building. (D.Thompson)

14.	The main hall is of generous proportions and has good catering provision. After less than ten years use, new ticket offices were provided and are seen on opening day, 17th June 1999. (M.J.Stretton)

OXFORD SHED

15. "Bulldog" class no. 3385 *Newport* stands alongside the coal stage during manual loading on 9th April 1927. A new double-sided stage was built in 1944, north of the turntable, but tubs and shovels were still used. (H.C.Casserley)

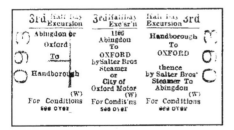

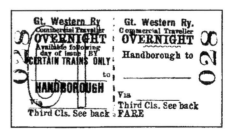

16.   Standing outside the former WMR shed on 7th September 1947 is "Metro Tank" no. 3585. On the right is the lifting shop for heavy repairs, such as axlebox replacement. The wagon is being loaded with ash, a major task at such depots. At its peak, the depot had 60 locomotives. (Millbrook House)

17.   The lifting shop in the background had a 50-ton hoist provided in 1931 when the building was extended. Behind no. 7911 *Lady Margaret Hall* on 21st March 1954 is ex-GWR railcar no. W3W. The 24,000 gallon water tank outlived the building by over 20 years. (P.Glenn)

18.   The haze prevents locomotive identification in this view from about 1963. On the left is the original single road shed erected by the OWWR. The steam shed closed on 3rd January 1966, its code being 81F. It was demolished in 1968. (J.H.Moss/R.S.Carpenter)

19.   Diesel locomotives were based and refuelled here until August 1984, but devoid of a building. No. 31143 is waiting between turns on 23rd February 1985, while Mk I coaches stand near one of the four carriage sidings. The pit is a legacy from steam days. (M.Turvey)

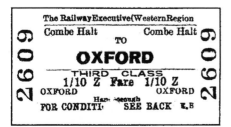

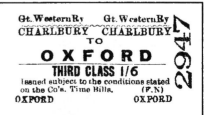

20.   A southbound freight passes Oxford North Junction box behind which are the former LNWR lines from Bicester and Bletchley. The locomotive is no. 5902 *Howick Hall*. Beyond the leading wagons are the connections between the two routes. These links supplemented the original exchange sidings near the station, the lines coming into use, along with the box, on 1st November 1940 to facilitate wartime traffic. Closure of both was on 29th October 1973, when the junction for the then singled line to Bicester was moved ½ mile north. (Unknown)

21.   This water tank is the only obvious item common to this and the previous photograph. The bridge in the latter was this photographer's viewpoint, sometime in 1958. No. 7315 is a 4300 class 2-6-0 and is working a stopping train, while coal arrives on the right and freight transfers from the London Midland Region to the Western on the left. (P.Q.Treloar)

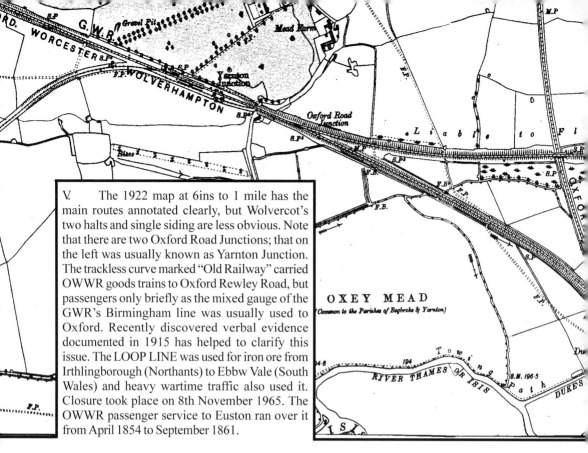

V. The 1922 map at 6ins to 1 mile has the main routes annotated clearly, but Wolvercot's two halts and single siding are less obvious. Note that there are two Oxford Road Junctions; that on the left was usually known as Yarnton Junction. The trackless curve marked "Old Railway" carried OWWR goods trains to Oxford Rewley Road, but passengers only briefly as the mixed gauge of the GWR's Birmingham line was usually used to Oxford. Recently discovered verbal evidence documented in 1915 has helped to clarify this issue. The LOOP LINE was used for iron ore from Irthlingborough (Northants) to Ebbw Vale (South Wales) and heavy wartime traffic also used it. Closure took place on 8th November 1965. The OWWR passenger service to Euston ran over it from April 1854 to September 1861.

22. A northward panorama from the same bridge has (from left to right) the down goods loop (1942-62), down main, no. 5012 *Berry Pomeroy Castle* with an inter-regional express, behind which is Port Meadow box and the LMR quadruple track, both 1940-61. Few footpaths crossed so many tracks. (P.Q.Treloar)

23. A southward view from 2002 has the four Turbo stabling sidings of 1992 on the left, followed by the up through siding, a signal, the two main lines, the reversible down goods line and the four overgrown and little used down carriage sidings. Ten Thames Turbos were normally berthed on the left each night. (V.Mitchell)

24.　　Wolvercot Siding was a short loop and carries a wagon on the right of this photograph of no. 7007 *Great Western* with a down Worcester express in November 1952. The roof of Wolvercot Siding box is above the fifth coach and the wartime down loop is on the extreme right. (J.B.Snell)

25.   Turning round, we see the connection between the 1942 down loop and the down main line, also the bridge between Upper and Lower Wolvercot. No. 3722 is on a trip from Yarnton to Hinksey Yard in about 1953. (J.B.Snell)

VI.   The 1914 survey features the siding which was accessed from the east by a bridge over the Oxford Canal and a level crossing over the running lines. The box and siding both closed on 9th June 1958. The siding had been used by a paper mill.

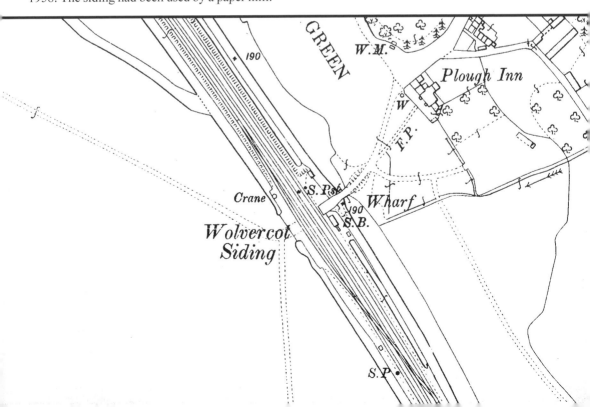

26.   The GWR's Wolvercot Halt was close to the lock on the Oxford Canal. Passengers were conveyed between 1st February 1908 and 1st January 1916, steam railmotors being usually employed. (Lens of Sutton)

27.   No. 4091 *Dudley Castle* brings a train from Worcester onto the main line from Birmingham on 14th June 1954. The down loop was closed on 29th October 1973, but the connections to both loops had been moved further south in 1966. Wolvercot Junction box had 35 levers and closed with the down loop. It was demolished in 1975. (J.B.Snell)

28.   The relay room was built near the site of the signal box and beyond it is the line to Worcester, which was singled as far as Ascott-under-Wychwood on 29th November 1971. All trains from Worcester use the crossover featured in this photograph, which was taken in March 2003. (V.Mitchell)

YARNTON

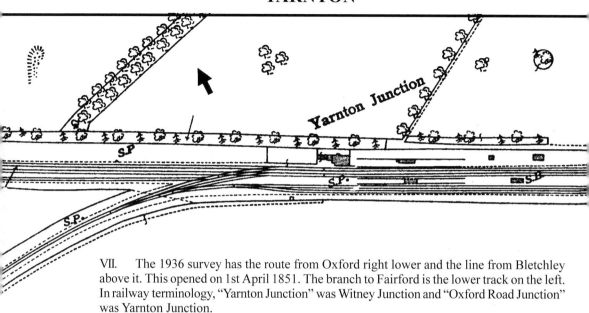

VII.   The 1936 survey has the route from Oxford right lower and the line from Bletchley above it. This opened on 1st April 1851. The branch to Fairford is the lower track on the left. In railway terminology, "Yarnton Junction" was Witney Junction and "Oxford Road Junction" was Yarnton Junction.

29.   In the distance is the Oxford Road Junction shown on the left page of map V. This and the next view are from the signal box in 1934. The local population rose from 280 in 1901 to 1371 in 1961. (Brunel University/Mowat coll.)

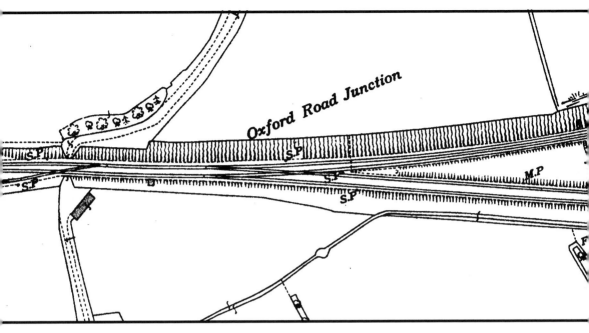

30.   The station opened with the branch on 13th November 1861 and the down platform was initially used as an island, but the left face was later fenced off. The line on the left had a point inserted in August 1940 to serve nine exchange sidings laid out in the field on the left.
(Brunel University/Mowat coll.)

31.   The unusually ornate down platform shelter is evident on 31st August 1952 as ex-MSWJR 2-4-0 no. 1335 is about to propel its railtour to Oxford Road Junction, having just run round its train. It started from Oxford and had run to Shipston-on-Stour and back; it ran forward to Oxford after traversing the Yarnton Loop. (H.C.Casserley)

32.   The junction for the Fairford branch was recorded on 24th April 1955 and is also shown in *Branch Line to Fairford*. The signals allowed access to the loop and thence the exchange sidings. From there trains ran regularly to such places as Cambridge, Wellingborough and Northampton at that period. (N.Simmons)

33.   The original building seen in picture 30 had gone by the time that this photograph was taken in May 1956, but the cast iron urinal remained. To the left of the nameboard are wagons in the exchange sidings. These had handled heavy traffic to and from US Air Force bases during and after World War II. A turntable was provided at the end of the nearest siding. (H.C.Casserley)

34.   The box opened on 13th June 1909 and replaced two situated at the adjacent junctions. It was all electrically operated at 120 volts, power being from batteries charged by a motor twice weekly. The advanced 50-lever system was abandoned in 1927 and the box closed on 28th March 1971 housing a conventional 51-lever frame. (Lens of Sutton coll.)

35.   No. 6924 *Grantley Hall* is seen on 7th June 1960 approaching the station, which closed on 18th June 1962. The branch lost its passenger service on the same day, but freight continued to Witney until 2nd November 1970. (D.A.Johnson)

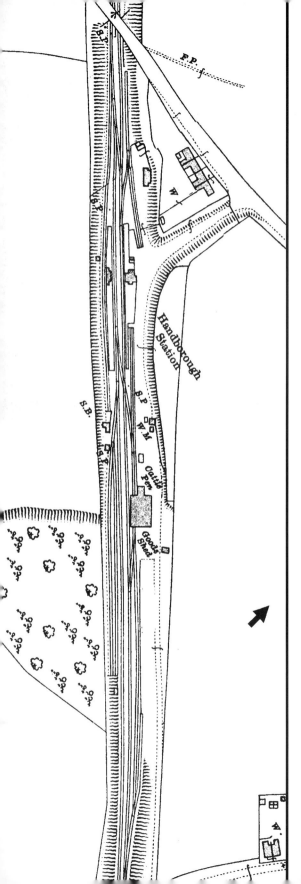

HANBOROUGH

36. The sign stated HANDBOROUGH JUNCTION long after 1861 and the refreshment room also remained. HANBOROUGH was the name used from 28th September 1992. Blenheim appeared on the name board, but this had a nearer station at Woodstock from 1890. (Lens of Sutton)

←

VIII. The track was doubled to here on 18th November 1853 and westwards in 1854. It was termed a junction when trains divided for Euston and Oxford between April 1854 and September 1861. The map from 1921 does not include the up refuge siding, which was beyond the bridge until 1965.

37. No details are available of this GWR down train. However record survives of the 5.0pm from Euston being combined here with the 6.30 from Paddington between July and September 1861, following the introduction of GWR standard gauge trains from the capital. The locomotive is one of the 3521 class, which were originally built in 1887 as 0-4-4Ts. (Lens of Sutton)

38. A footbridge was authorised in 1914, but never provided. The village had 879 residents in 1901 and so there were never large crowds using the barrow crossings. There was a staff of six for most of the 1930s. (LGRP/NRM)

Handborough	1903	1913	1923	1933
Passenger tickets issued	13681	14351	13805	12285
Season tickets issued	*	*	251	852
Parcels forwarded	4147	5081	9949	2894
General goods forwarded (tons)	1637	1477	1619	849
Coal and coke received (tons)	41	103	173	63
Other minerals received (tons)	1483	1398	1327	706
General goods received (tons)	3468	2466	1539	609
Trucks of livestock handled	72	90	222	37

(* not available.)

Gt. Western Ry.   Gt. Western Ry.

Moreton-in-Marsh   Moreton-in-Marsh

TO

OXFORD

2/4 PARLY. (3rd Cls.) 2/4

Issued subject to the conditions an regulations set out in the Company Time Tables books and Bills.   (HG

OXFORD   OXFORD

5410

39.   As at Yarnton, the down platform was probably used as an island during the junction era. The goods shed housed a 30cwt crane. (LGRP/NRM)

40.　　The refuge sidings on the right would have been of value as exchange sidings prior to the opening of Yarnton. LNWR locomotives did not run west of here. We have found no reference to a turntable and so they presumably turned on the triangle north of Wolvercot. (LGRP/NRM)

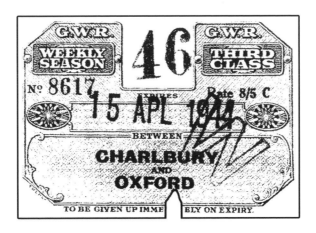

41.   We can now enjoy three photographs from 19th October 1957, taken in low sunlight. In unusually clean condition, 2-8-0 no. 2899 passes through with assorted freight wagons. (R.M.Casserley)

42.   The station received national attention on 30th January 1965 when Southern Region 4-6-2 no. 34051 *Winston Churchill* brought the body of that great statesman here for burial at nearby Bladon. Blenheim Palace was his ancestral home, but the Woodstock branch had closed in 1954. A temporary facing crossover was provided for the funeral train. (R.M.Casserley)

43.   The signal box was in use from 1884 until 22nd June 1966 and had 42 levers. The goods yard closed on 13th September 1965 and passing it is 2-6-2T no. 5170. (R.M.Casserley)

44.   A Brush Type 4 speeds through on 26th June 1965, the rear coaches being near sidings laid on the up side during World War II for the Ministry of Food. Known as Becks Siding, they lasted until 1966. The posts are fitted with winches for pressurised oil lamps made by Tilley. (P.J.Kelley)

45.   Only the up platform remained in use after 1971 and it had been resurfaced by the time that this photograph was taken on 11th April 1991. The train is the 08.50 from Oxford. The station is adjacent to the fine Oxford Bus Museum, making it easily accessible to those interested in road transport history. (M.J.Stretton)

COMBE

46.   The staggered wooden platforms came into use on 8th July 1935 and were known as "Combe Halt" until 1969. Since January 1966, only one train each weekday has stopped. Details are given in caption 53. (R.M.Casserley)

IX.   The private siding served the Duke of Marlborough's estate from at least 1872 until 1955 and is seen on the 1921 map. It was a little to the west of the later halt. A further mile down the line was Fawler Siding, which carried iron ore from nearby pits probably in 1859-66 and 1874-90. The siding was a trailing one on the up side. Inset is a 2003 photo of one of the smallest stations in the area.

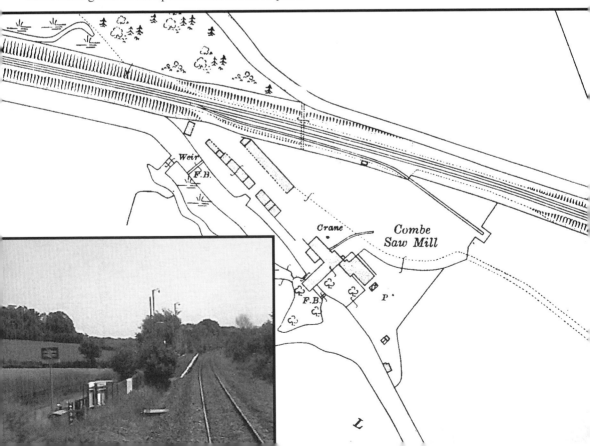

WEST OF COMBE

47.   No. 50029 roars through the Oxfordshire countryside with the 08.05 Hereford to Paddington service on 2nd July 1983. The class 50 diesels were introduced in 1967. (P.G.Barnes)

FINSTOCK

48.   This 1959 view towards Oxford includes both of the inclined footways to the platforms, which came into use on 9th April 1934. (R.M.Casserley)

49.   The down side waiting room would accommodate a good crowd, but there were only 451 residents in 1901. The figure increased by 16 in the following 60 years. (N.Simmons)

50.   No. 6163 approaches with the 5.37pm from Oxford on 18th July 1959. This called at all stations to Kingham, except Yarnton. Three other down trains stopped here at that time. (H.C.Casserley)

51.   Beyer Peacock Hymek diesel hydraulic no. D7009 heads the 10.35 Hereford to Paddington and passes through on 16th April 1965. (M.Mensing/M.J.Stretton)

52.	No. 47055 speeds through with the 16.03 from Worcester en route to London on 26th September 1980. This platform lasted until 9th March 1987, when a new one came into use on the opposite side of the line. (T.Heavyside)

53.	Seen from the same viewpoint on 27th February 1999 is the 09.44 Hereford to Paddington, formed of Thames Turbo no. 166213. There was one train calling each way; by 2003 it was timed at 08.00 to Oxford and at 18.41 in the down direction, on Mondays to Fridays. (M.J.Stretton)

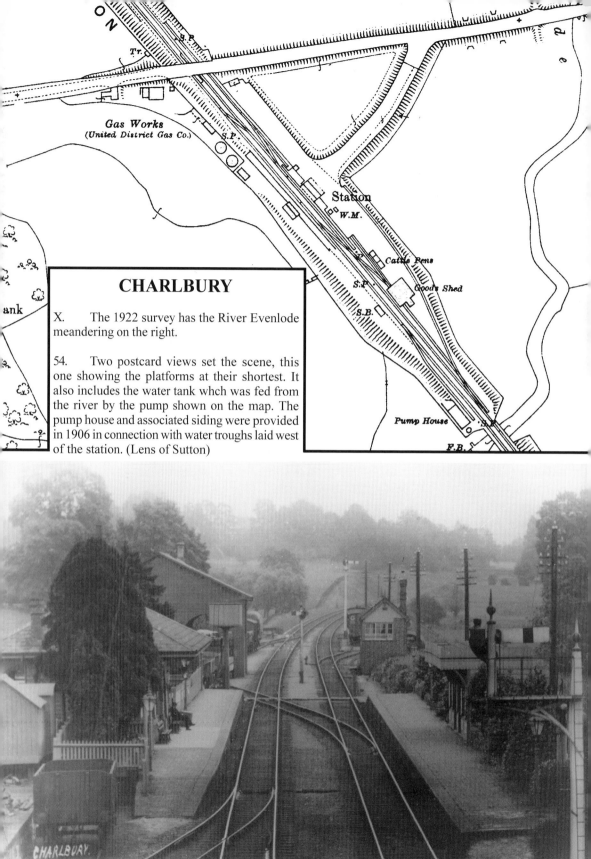

CHARLBURY

X.   The 1922 survey has the River Evenlode meandering on the right.

54.   Two postcard views set the scene, this one showing the platforms at their shortest. It also includes the water tank whch was fed from the river by the pump shown on the map. The pump house and associated siding were provided in 1906 in connection with water troughs laid west of the station. (Lens of Sutton)

55.　　A delightfully posed view includes the blue chequered pattern bricks standardised for GWR platforms. The population increased by only 300 in the 60 years from 1901, when it was 1352. (Lens of Sutton)

56.　　Probably from about 1925, this panorama shows that only the down platform could be lengthened. This was carried out in 1928. On the right is the gasworks, the coal for which had to be conveyed in a cart from the left of the picture. There were eight men employed at this station between the two world wars. (LGRP/NRM)

BRITISH RLYS (W)	BRITISH RLYS (W)
CHARLBURY	CHARLBURY
TO	
FINSTOCK HALT	
THIRD CLASS	
5½d. Z Fare 5½d. Z	
Finstock	Finstock
FOR CONDITIONS	FOR CONDITIONS
SEE BACK.	SEE BACK (W.L

1659   1659

O. W. & W. R.
SHIPTON TO
CHARLBURY
FIRST CLASS.
THIS TICKET IS ISSUED, SUBJECT TO THE
CONDITIONS STATED IN THE COS. TIME TABLE

CB 83

Charlbury	1903	1913	1923	1933
Passenger tickets issued	18844	18061	17206	15768
Season tickets issued	*	*	392	533
Parcels forwarded	14497	19079	15731	14525
General goods forwarded (tons)	3823	3510	3300	1869
Coal and coke received (tons)	306	657	701	126
Other minerals received (tons)	1976	1705	3873	2052
General goods received (tons)	3949	3787	3034	1999
Trucks of livestock handled	166	444	387	82

(* not available.)

57.   The siding on the right had been lengthened in about 1885 to give better access to the coal wharf. Sugg's shadow-free Rochester lamps had replaced their Windsor pattern.
(Lens of Sutton coll.)

58. GWR railcars were in use from 1934 until 1962, this example being recorded in 1957. This is one of the first batch of 16, which were built with miniature buffers. (S.J.Dickson)

59. Brunel's chalet style building is seen to good advantage in this photo fronm July 1959. The goods shed had a 30cwt crane, but freight service was withdrawn on 2nd November 1970. The 34-lever signal box closed with the singling on 29th November 1971. (H.C.Casserley)

60.   The exterior was photographed in 1979 and the structure was listed soon after for preservation for posterity. All regular services stopped here from 1966 and only one platform was needed after 1971. (P.J.Kelley)

61.   The 15.00 Paddington to Hereford was hauled by no. 47466 on 26th September 1980. The open wires on porcelain insulators would soon be displaced by insulated ones in the ducting. (T.Heavyside)

62.   The platform was not lengthened as most trains became shorter. An example is seen on 2nd July 1983 and seldom were there more than four coaches after 1992, although one service on weekdays was provided by an HST. The station was highly commended in the Small Stations Awards of 1996-97 and it still had a ticket office, which was staffed on weekday mornings. (P.G.Barnes)

EAST OF
ASCOTT-UNDER-WYCHWOOD

63. "Castle" class no. 7000 *Viscount Portal* hauled the down "Cathedrals Express" on Whit Monday, 3rd June 1963. It was recorded about half a mile from the station. (M.Mensing/M.J.Stretton)

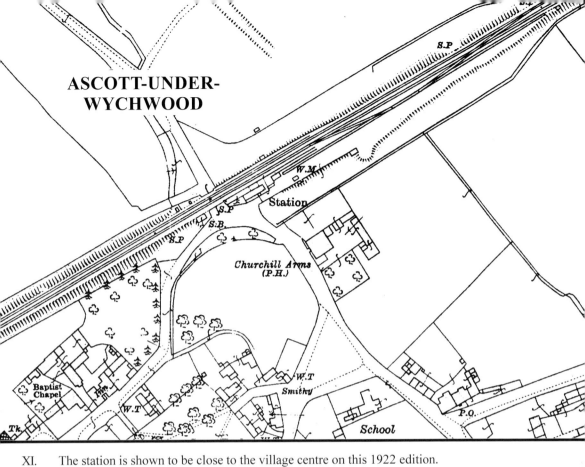

ASCOTT-UNDER-WYCHWOOD

XI.   The station is shown to be close to the village centre on this 1922 edition.

64.   There would have been little demand for this postcard as there were only 372 inhabitants recorded in 1901. Total value of tickets sold was only £392 in 1903. (Lens of Sutton)

65.   A lengthy goods train is held at the down starting signal, sometime before red targets were fitted to level crossing gates. (Lens of Sutton)

66.   The single siding is included in this view from about 1930, at which time there were five employees. There had been a second short siding near the platform until about 1916. (Brunel University/Mowat coll.)

67.   This photo includes the approach to the goods yard and the well protected entrance to the station. The date of 18th July 1959 applies to this and the next two pictures. (H.C.Casserley)

Ascott-under-Wychwood	1903	1913	1923	1933
Passenger tickets issued	5232	4641	4500	5423
Season tickets issued	*	*	14	71
Parcels forwarded	2554	3685	3692	1590
General goods forwarded (tons)	868	670	378	117
Coal and coke received (tons)	18	33	55	-
Other minerals received (tons)	17	645	595	284
General goods received (tons)	320	734	441	254
Trucks of livestock handled	-	-	-	-
(* not available.)				

68.   To the left of the non-pressurised oil lamp is the gate to the up platform and to the right is a wicket gate that could be used by pedestrians when the main gates were closed across the road. The wickets were controlled by two dedicated levers in the box. (R.M.Casserley)

⟶

69.   This view towards Oxford includes the points to the goods yard, which closed on 13th September 1965, but less obvious is a crossover beyond them. The siding remained until the mid eighties. Staffing ceased on 24th May 1965, when the term "halt" was applied. It was dropped on 5th May 1969. (H.C.Casserley)

⟶

70.   The 1884 signal box was still in use when photographed in March 2003 and was the only intermediate one on the route. A 25-lever frame had been installed in 1949 and full lifting barriers came into use on 26th November 1976. The single line was worked by a system of axle counters, instead of tokens. (V.Mitchell)

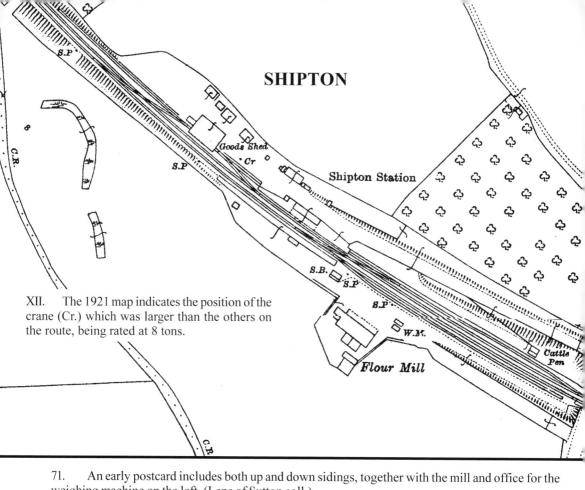

SHIPTON

Goods Shed

Shipton Station

Flour Mill

XII.   The 1921 map indicates the position of the crane (Cr.) which was larger than the others on the route, being rated at 8 tons.

71.   An early postcard includes both up and down sidings, together with the mill and office for the weighing machine on the left. (Lens of Sutton coll.)

72.   The staff numbered 14 in 1913, but there is no record of the date of this varied group, which includes two of the large milk churns and a shunting pole. (Lens of Sutton coll.)

73.   By 1938, there were 20 employees here and so the coach was presumably provided as extra staff accommodation. A 21-lever frame was fitted in the 1884 signal box in 1940 and it remained in use until 12th October 1965. (LGRP/NRM)

74.   Photographed in April 1962, the station had lost its canopy, but gained a parcels shed. The goods service ceased on 13th September 1965 and staff were withdrawn on 3rd January 1966. It was described as a halt from that time until 5th May 1969. (P.J.Garland/R.S.Carpenter)

75.   Little remained to record in March 2003 and the service was down to one train on weekdays from each platform. Shipton-under-Wychwood housed 672 souls in 1901 and 775 in 1961. Wychwood Forest once stretched from here to Charlbury. (V.Mitchell)

WEST OF SHIPTON

76.   Bruern Crossing carries the lane between Lyneham and Bruern Abbey and is seen in March 1971 as class 47 no. 1953 approaches with an up train issuing steam from a parcels van. (J.H.Bird)

77.   The box was a block post until 31st October 1971. Full lifting barriers came into use that day, but the box continued to be manned until 25th November 1973. (J.H.Bird)

Shipton	1903	1913	1923	1933
Passenger tickets issued	15296	13229	10072	5880
Season tickets issued	*	*	14	206
Parcels forwarded	16460	18046	19716	12160
General goods forwarded (tons)	4088	5037	4615	4370
Coal and coke received (tons)	316	366	641	388
Other minerals received (tons)	1817	4006	3479	2038
General goods received (tons)	4011	4579	4115	2470
Trucks of livestock handled	216	326	186	49

(* not available.)

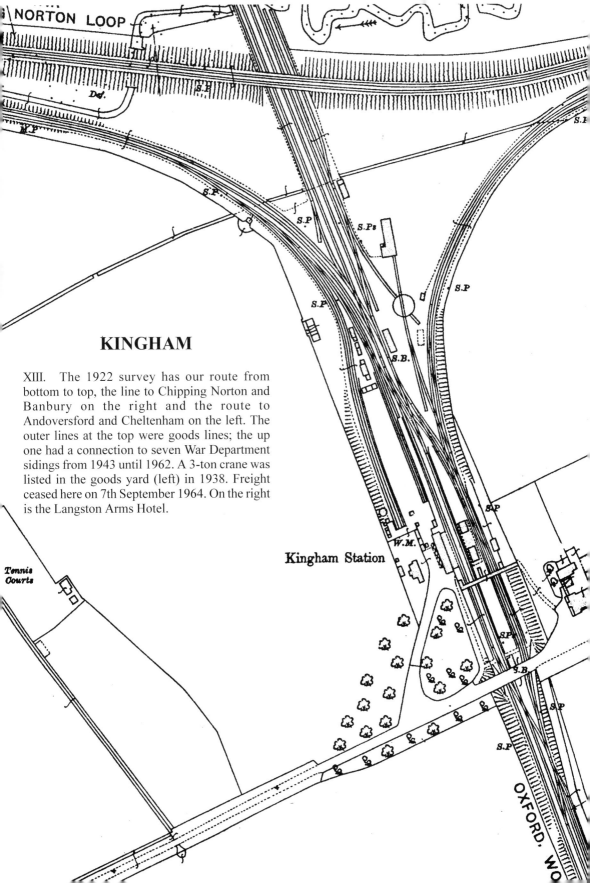

NORTON LOOP

Def.

S.P.

M.P.

S.P.

S.P.

S.Ps

S.P

S.P

S.P

S.B.

KINGHAM

XIII. The 1922 survey has our route from bottom to top, the line to Chipping Norton and Banbury on the right and the route to Andoversford and Cheltenham on the left. The outer lines at the top were goods lines; the up one had a connection to seven War Department sidings from 1943 until 1962. A 3-ton crane was listed in the goods yard (left) in 1938. Freight ceased here on 7th September 1964. On the right is the Langston Arms Hotel.

W.M.

S.P

Kingham Station

Tennis Courts

S.P

S.B.

S.P

S.P

OXFORD. WO

78.   This postcard was produced when the station was called "Chipping Norton Junction", a name that was in use until 1st May 1909. This northward view includes a train signalled for Chipping Norton. The steps of South Box are on the left; this closed in 1922 and is shown on the map. (Lens of Sutton)

79.   A view from the road bridge includes the water column used for refreshing locomotives arriving from Cheltenham or Banbury. The nearby village of Kingham had only 816 residents in 1901. (Lens of Sutton)

80.   The ridge of the Cotswolds is in the background and surrounding the station are the pastures which generated the milk to fill the numerous churns included in this view. They were labour intensive and there were over 20 men here until 1931, when bulk transport of milk was becoming common. (LGRP/NRM)

Kingham	1903	1913	1923	1933
Passenger tickets issued	21925	21071	22629	9112
Season tickets issued	*	*	52	43
Parcels forwarded	14394	16061	23063	13385
General goods forwarded (tons)	1416	1120	1043	512
Coal and coke received (tons)	49	87	124	36
Other minerals received (tons)	1299	901	757	726
General goods received (tons)	1749	1588	1217	497
Trucks of livestock handled	281	369	495	205

(* not available.)

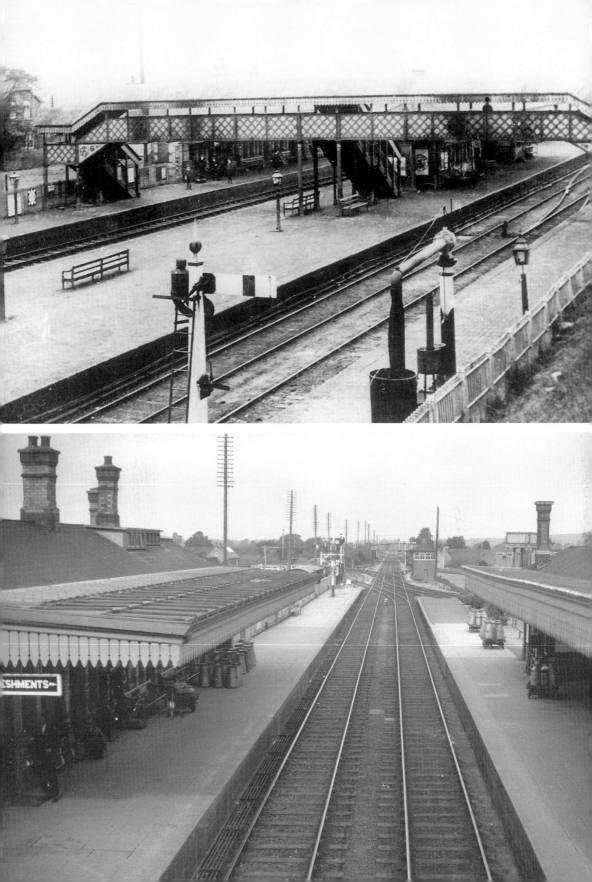

81.   The 1906 bridge for the Cheltenham-Banbury direct line is in the background and the goods loops are below it. The cross country stopping trains used the platforms in the foreground. (LGRP/NRM)

82.   The buildings date from a rebuild of 1883 and offered good facilities for those changing trains here. Two local services call to exchange a few patient travellers. (Lens of Sutton coll.)

83.   No. 5034 *Corfe Castle* brakes the 4.0pm Worcester to Paddington on 18th July 1959. By this time, electric lighting had arrived, further reducing labour requirements. The double track over the bridge was not used after 1953, although one line was retained for engine turning until 1961. Earlier it had carried many trains of iron ore from the Midlands to South Wales. (H.C.Casserley)

84.   No. 5090 *Neath Abbey* was relegated to a short stopping train on 8th March 1961. The signal box had 91 levers and was in use until 24th July 1966, the branch lines having closed to passengers in 1962 and goods in 1964. The name North Box was used from 1906 until 1922. (M.A.N.Johnston)

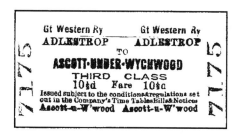

Gt Western Ry   Gt Western Ry
ADLESTROP   ADLESTROP
TO
ASCOTT-UNDER-WYCHWOOD
THIRD   CLASS
10½d   Fare   10½d
Issued subject to the conditions&regulations set
out in the Company's Time Tables Bills&Notices
Ascott-u-W'wood   Ascott-u-W'wood

KINGHAM
CHANGE for CHIPPING NORTON
BOURTON-ON-WATER
& CHELTENHAM &c

85.   A 3-car Swindon Cross Country DMU was working the 1.20pm Oxford to Moreton-in-Marsh on 2nd September 1961 and was towing two four-wheeled vans. On most weekdays, there were four stopping trains, two of which terminated here. (M.Mensing/M.J.Stretton)

86.   Two sidings diverged into the field on the right during World War II. The horse dock is visible above no. 7004 *Eastnor Castle* as it runs in at 5.8pm with the 3.15pm Paddington to Hereford on 17th August 1962. Such expresses were at two hour intervals, but the stopping trains were less frequent. (L.W.Rowe)

87.   On the right is the locomotive shed, which was in use from 1913 to 1962. It had a 44ft turntable for some years. On the left are parts of the extensive cattle pens. There had been a smaller engine shed in the same area from 1881 to 1906; it had only a 22ft turntable. (L.W.Rowe)

88.   The station was still largely intact when photographed in March 1971 as no. D7030 arrived with the 11.15 Paddington to Worcester. The train service had been halved in 1966 and regular travellers from Stow-on-the Wold were outraged. At this period, there were four other fast trains from London, plus one that called at all stations after Oxford. (J.H.Bird)

89.   A so-called Super Sprinter creeps into the desolate platforms, forming the 10.57 Hereford to Oxford on 27th October 1989. The traditional nameboards had been provided by the Cotswold Line Promotion Group. The next two photos are from the same day. (M.J.Stretton)

90.   The tracks through the platforms on the right remained in place until July 1966. The amputated roofless footbridge and general dereliction did little to attract passengers. A ticket office was still in use on the down side in the mornings in 2003. (M.J.Stretton)

91. At least there was a small shelter on the up side and it is seen as the 13.31 Worcester to Paddington called briefly to disturb the prolonged tranquility at this remote location. (M.J.Stretton)

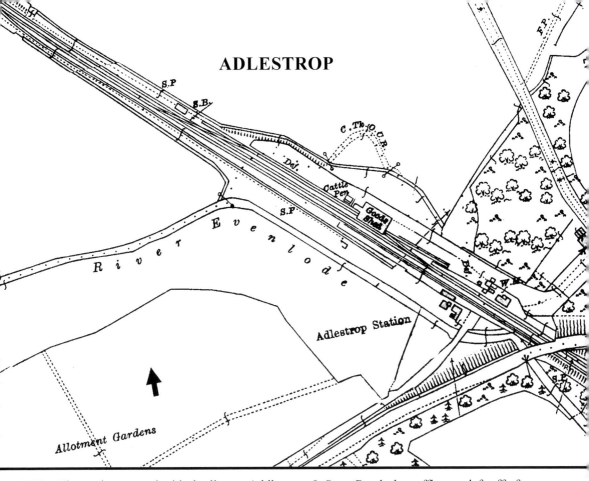

ADLESTROP

XIV.   The station opened with the line as Addlestrop & Stow Road; the suffix was left off after March 1862 and one d was dropped in July 1883. The map is from 1921 and shows the proximity of the river.

92.   A westward view includes the substantial station house. There were four men here up to 1923, but the figure dropped to two by 1933. The peacefulness of the location in June 1898 inspired Edward Thomas to pen his famous poem about an express that "drew up unwantedly" one Summer afternoon. The population was 190 in 1901. (Lens of Sutton coll.)

93.   The main entrance was between the poster offering holidays in Britain in 1933 and a trip to Barry. There were four weekdays trains each way at this period, plus two on Sundays. The goods shed had a one-ton crane, but a crane arrived between two bolster wagons when timber had to be loaded. The down refuge siding is on the left. (Lens of Sutton coll.)

94.   Two photographs from 27th June 1959 include most details except the lamps. However, the lamp room is the shed on the left. Trains calling each weekday at that time were at 8.9am and 7.22pm down and at 7.34, 9.12, and 11.42am up. (P.J.Garland/R.S.Carpenter)

95.   The signal box had 25 levers, was completed in 1906 and was normally only used during shunting. It closed on 27th April 1964, goods traffic having ceased here on 29th August 1963. The station closed completely on 3rd January 1966; one seat survived, being transferred to the local bus shelter. (P.J.Garland/R.S.Carpenter)

Adlestrop	1903	1913	1923	1933
Passenger tickets issued	5996	5492	4715	2160
Season tickets issued	*	*	56	52
Parcels forwarded	6237	12168	9349	1976
General goods forwarded (tons)	1212	1129	620	164
Coal and coke received (tons)	116	73	167	51
Other minerals received (tons)	675	675	826	749
General goods received (tons)	496	604	668	159
Trucks of livestock handled	88	73	118	38
(* not available.)				

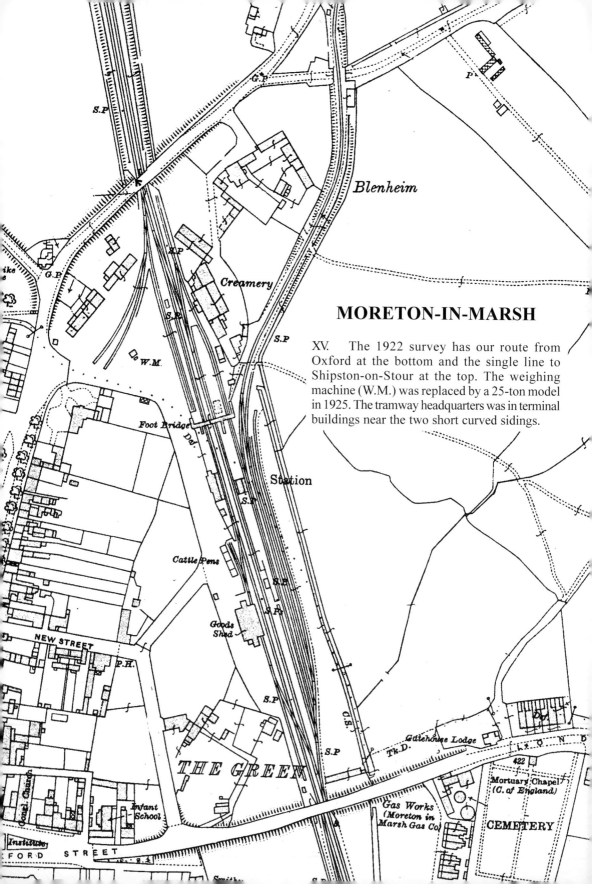

MORETON-IN-MARSH

XV.   The 1922 survey has our route from Oxford at the bottom and the single line to Shipston-on-Stour at the top. The weighing machine (W.M.) was replaced by a 25-ton model in 1925. The tramway headquarters was in terminal buildings near the two short curved sidings.

Blenheim

Creamery

Station

Foot Bridge

Cattle Pens

Goods Shed

NEW STREET

P.H.

THE GREEN

Infant School

FORD STREET

Gatehouse Lodge

Mortuary Chapel (C. of England)

CEMETERY

Gas Works (Moreton in Marsh Gas Co)

422

Cong. Church

Institute

96.   New buildings were erected in 1872-73 and this picture appears to show the work nearing completion. There was a staff of 18 in 1903, this rising to 20 in the 1920s. (Lens of Sutton)

97.   A "Dean Goods" 0-6-0 is seen in action between the two world wars; some were in military service in both wars. In the background is the crane, which was rated at six tons. (A.W.V.Mace/Mile Post 92½)

98.   The vans on the left are standing at the creamery platform, while those on the right are at a dock for public traffic. The sidings leading from the right of the picture were near the site of the 1826 tramway terminus. (Lens of Sutton)

99.   The Stratford & Moreton Tramway terminus comprised offices, workshops, stables and living accommodation. The solid structure stood for over 120 years. (Lens of Sutton)

100.   The branch platform is on the right, the lack of a white edging suggesting that it is out of use, services having ceased in 1929. An obliging porter is taking cases over the track. (Lens of Sutton)

Moreton-in-Marsh	1903	1913	1923	1933
Passenger tickets issued	28682	29443	24862	16969
Season tickets issued	*	*	165	53
Parcels forwarded	46605	34722	80626	161851
General goods forwarded (tons)	5458	4621	3980	687
Coal and coke received (tons)	751	631	1133	230
Other minerals received (tons)	3624	3459	4556	6292
General goods received (tons)	4353	4715	4035	4037
Trucks of livestock handled	415	599	519	278
(* not available.)				

101.   A 1956 view features the intricate porch and the complex footbridge, which had four flights of steps as one pair served a public footpath - see map. The nearest door is for the station master; by 2003, the office was used by a cycle hire company. (Lens of Sutton)

→

102.   No. 4088 *Dartmouth Castle* runs in with a Worcester to Paddington service on 11th October 1958, all the coaches gleaming as well. There were seven expresses to London on weekdays at that time, with two on Sundays.
(H.F.Wheeller/R.S.Carpenter)

→

103.   The long disused cattle dock is on the left as the 13.30 Hereford to Reading departs on 6th April 1982. The signal box had a 40-lever frame and was still in use in 2003. Electric tokens were in use westwards on the single line to Evesham. (T.Heavyside)

104.   No. 47831 was recorded with the diverted 09.15 Poole to Glasgow Central on 14th July 1996. The wide track spacing is a legacy of the broad gauge fiasco in which vast sums of money were wasted. (P.G.Barnes)

105.   The 12.45 from Paddington is about to leave for Great Malvern on 30th March 1996. With sidings and semaphores, the station provided a nostalgic link with the past, even if the trains did not. (N.Sprinks)

106.   Although modernised, the footbridge still had a complicated pattern of steps, but the up platform had only a simple shelter. The overgrown engineers siding was all that remained of the branch to Shipston-on-Stour. No. 166213 is working the 10.03 Great Malvern to Paddington on 14 July 1996. (P.G.Barnes)

Shipston-on-Stour Branch

STRETTON-ON-FOSSE

XVI.   The origin of the branch and the reason for its indirect alignment are evident. (Railway Magazine)

XVII.   The 1902 map includes the short siding, which was in use until freight service here was withdrawn on 1st June 1941. The road is the Roman Fosse Way, the A429 since 1919. Four men were employed here in 1923, but only one by 1929. The village housed 321 in 1901.

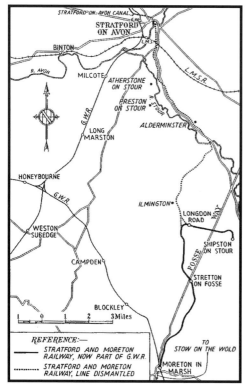

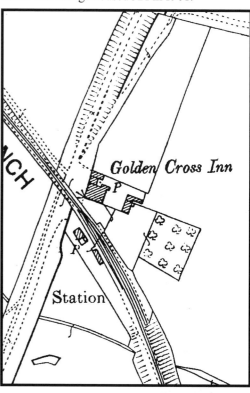

107.   Prior to 1917, three of the four trains called here by request although not shown in the timetable. There was no service in 1917-19, although trains had to stop because of the gates. (Lens of Sutton)

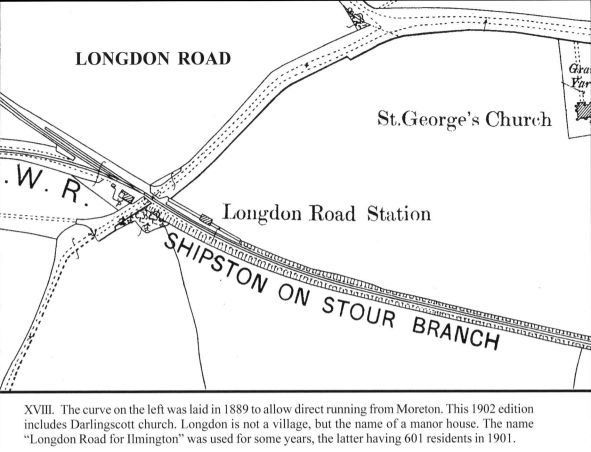

LONGDON ROAD

St.George's Church

.W.R.

Longdon Road Station

SHIPSTON ON STOUR BRANCH

XVIII. The curve on the left was laid in 1889 to allow direct running from Moreton. This 1902 edition includes Darlingscott church. Longdon is not a village, but the name of a manor house. The name "Longdon Road for Ilmington" was used for some years, the latter having 601 residents in 1901.

108.   Two photographs from 29th April 1934 include the remaining part of the route to Stratford-upon-Avon, probably used by market day wagons until 1900. The siding was closed to traffic on 1st June 1941. (Brunel University/Clinker coll.)

109.   The track was kept clear up as far as this gate and used as a second siding until 1941. Both were removed in 1948, but fortunately had been recorded by these serious students of railways. (Brunel University/Clinker coll.)

110.   This 1934 view includes the 1902 goods shed beyond the main building. A staff of three was provided in 1903, 1913 and 1923, but only one man in 1929-30. It was unusual to find a loading gauge on a running line, even a goods one. (LGRP/NRM)

111.   A photo from the 1950s includes the former junction area, seen in picture 108. A horse loading dock was added in 1899, its location being still evident in the background. (D.Lawrence)

Stretton-on-Fosse	1903	1913	1923	1933
Passenger tickets issued	2589	2631	1814	-
Season tickets issued	*	*	-	-
Parcels forwarded	1224	2799	1700	276
General goods forwarded (tons)	167	522	90	27
Coal and coke received (tons)	8	12	-	-
Other minerals received (tons)	109	630	2617	63
General goods received (tons)	75	202	225	25
Trucks of livestock handled	-	-	-	-

(* not available.)

Longdon Road	1903	1913	1923	1933
Passenger tickets issued	2931	2580	1447	-
Season tickets issued	*	*	4	-
Parcels forwarded	687	2269	670	446
General goods forwarded (tons)	347	428	271	52
Coal and coke received (tons)	14	48	17	31
Other minerals received (tons)	770	1985	1603	238
General goods received (tons)	133	332	274	113
Trucks of livestock handled	1	1	-	2

(* not available.)

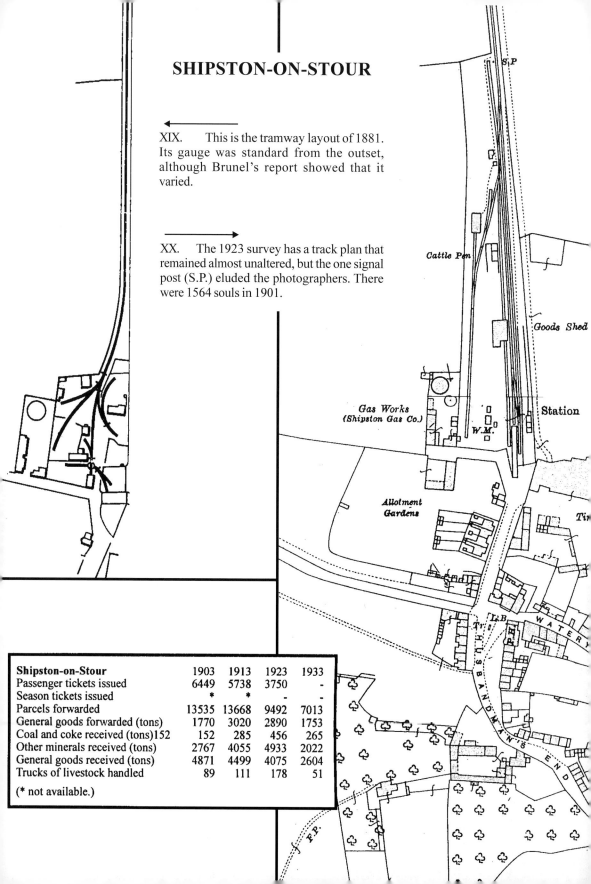

SHIPSTON-ON-STOUR

XIX.　This is the tramway layout of 1881. Its gauge was standard from the outset, although Brunel's report showed that it varied.

XX.　The 1923 survey has a track plan that remained almost unaltered, but the one signal post (S.P.) eluded the photographers. There were 1564 souls in 1901.

Cattle Pen

Goods Shed

Gas Works (Shipston Gas Co.)

Station

W.M.

Allotment Gardens

Shipston-on-Stour	1903	1913	1923	1933
Passenger tickets issued	6449	5738	3750	-
Season tickets issued	*	*	-	-
Parcels forwarded	13535	13668	9492	7013
General goods forwarded (tons)	1770	3020	2890	1753
Coal and coke received (tons)152	152	285	456	265
Other minerals received (tons)	2767	4055	4933	2022
General goods received (tons)	4871	4499	4075	2604
Trucks of livestock handled	89	111	178	51

(* not available.)

112.　　Two indifferent prints from 29th April 1934 are included as they show the general arrangement well. There was no signal box, the point rodding coming from a ground frame unlocked by a key on the single line staff. There were two such frames until February 1952. (Brunel University/Clinker coll.)

113.　　The rodding from South Ground Frame is included, as are the oil lamps which is surprising as passenger services ceased on 8th July 1929. However, 153 tickets were issued in 1930 and 9 in 1931, but we know not why. The loading dock on the left was added in 1914. (Brunel University/Clinker coll)

114.   We can now enjoy four good photographs taken in about 1949. The town's gas holder is visible beyond the cattle pens and the oil store is on the left. The shed had a crane capable of lifting 1 ton 15 cwt. (J.H.Moss/R.S.Carpenter)

115.   There were six men employed during most of the 1930s and goods traffic evidently was in excess of the capacity of the shed, necessitating the addition of two retired vans. (J.H.Moss/R.S.Carpenter)

116.   The engine shed ceased to be used for its intended purpose on 20th November 1916 and had its track removed in 1917. It later housed the GWR's lorry. (J.H.Moss/R.S.Carpenter)

117.   Goods service was withdrawn from the branch on 2nd May 1960, but the office and shed remained in use until 4th February 1963, as a NRCD - "Non Rail Connected Depot". (J.H.Moss/R.S.Carpenter)

118.   This and the next picture feature the afternoon tour run from Oxford on 31st August 1952, seen earlier in picture 31 at Yarnton. Apart from the effects of the late arrival of the weedkilling train, the track seems in fair order. (N.W.Sprinks)

119.   A relaxed atmosphere prevailed on railtours in the 1950s. Sister MSWJR loco no. 1336 was also used on such specials. Another was operated by the Railway Enthusiasts Club on 24th April 1955, using "Dean Goods" no. 2474. (H.C.Casserley)

120.   The paint was peeling, the buffer was split and the daily goods was down to two vans and a truck. This is the end of the branch and sadly the end of our quiet amble along it. (D.Lawrence)

XXI.   The tramway terminus at Stratford-upon-Avon is included for the sake of completeness. The site was not used for passenger traffic in the town after 1858. Its informal use for horse drawn wagons seems to have continued until about 1900. This was a reversion to the original arrangement whereby carriers provided their own wagons, as on the Surrey Iron Railway.

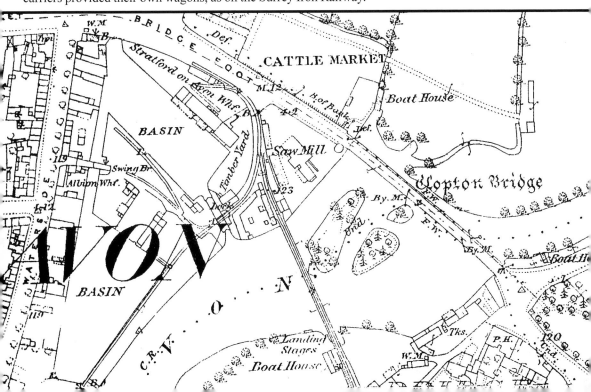

Middleton Press

Easebourne Lane, Midhurst, W Sussex. GU29 9AZ Tel: 01730 813169 Fax: 01730 812601
Email: sales@middletonpress.co.uk   www.middletonpress.co.uk
If books are not available from your local transport stockist, order direct post free UK.

BRANCH LINES
Branch Line to Allhallows
Branch Line to Alton
Branch Lines around Ascot
Branch Line to Ashburton
Branch Lines around Bodmin
Branch Line to Bude
Branch Lines around Canterbury
Branch Lines around Chard & Yeovil
Branch Line to Cheddar
Branch Lines around Cromer
Branch Line to the Derwent Valley
Branch Lines to East Grinstead
Branch Lines of East London
Branch Lines to Effingham Junction
Branch Lines around Exmouth
Branch Lines to Falmouth, Helston & St. Ives
Branch Line to Fairford
Branch Lines around Gosport
Branch Line to Hayling
Branch Lines to Henley, Windsor & Marlow
Branch Line to Hawkhurst
Branch Line to Horsham
Branch Lines around Huntingdon
Branch Line to Ilfracombe
Branch Line to Kingsbridge
Branch Line to Kingswear
Branch Line to Lambourn
Branch Lines to Launceston & Princetown
Branch Lines to Longmoor
Branch Line to Looe
Branch Line to Lyme Regis
Branch Line to Lynton
Branch Lines around March
Branch Lines around Midhurst
Branch Line to Minehead
Branch Line to Moretonhampstead
Branch Lines to Newport (IOW)
Branch Lines to Newquay
Branch Lines around North Woolwich
Branch Line to Padstow
Branch Lines around Plymouth
Branch Lines to Princes Risborough
Branch Lines to Seaton and Sidmouth
Branch Lines around Sheerness
Branch Line to Shrewsbury
Branch Line to Tenterden
Branch Lines around Tiverton
Branch Lines to Torrington
Branch Lines to Tunbridge Wells
Branch Line to Upwell
Branch Lines of West London
Branch Lines of West Wiltshire
Branch Lines around Weymouth
Branch Lines around Wimborne
Branch Lines around Wisbech

NARROW GAUGE
Austrian Narrow Gauge
Branch Line to Lynton
Branch Lines around Portmadoc 1923-46
Branch Lines around Porthmadog 1954-94
Branch Line to Southwold
Douglas to Port Erin
Douglas to Peel
Kent Narrow Gauge
Northern France Narrow Gauge
Romneyrail
Southern France Narrow Gauge
Sussex Narrow Gauge
Surrey Narrow Gauge
Swiss Narrow Gauge

Two-Foot Gauge Survivors
Vivarais Narrow Gauge

SOUTH COAST RAILWAYS
Ashford to Dover
Bournemouth to Weymouth
Brighton to Worthing
Dover to Ramsgate
Eastbourne to Hastings
Hastings to Ashford
Portsmouth to Southampton
Ryde to Ventnor
Southampton to Bournemouth

SOUTHERN MAIN LINES
Basingstoke to Salisbury
Crawley to Littlehampton
Dartford to Sittingbourne
East Croydon to Three Bridges
Epsom to Horsham
Exeter to Barnstaple
Exeter to Tavistock
Faversham to Dover
London Bridge to East Croydon
Orpington to Tonbridge
Tonbridge to Hastings
Salisbury to Yeovil
Sittingbourne to Ramsgate
Swanley to Ashford
Tavistock to Plymouth
Three Bridges to Brighton
Victoria to Bromley South
Victoria to East Croydon
Waterloo to Windsor
Waterloo to Woking
Woking to Portsmouth
Woking to Southampton
Yeovil to Exeter

EASTERN MAIN LINES
Barking to Southend
Ely to Kings Lynn
Ely to Norwich
Fenchurch Street to Barking
Hitchin to Peterborough
Ilford to Shenfield
Ipswich to Saxmundham
Liverpool Street to Ilford
Saxmundham to Yarmouth
Tilbury Loop

WESTERN MAIN LINES
Bristol to Taunton
Didcot to Banbury
Didcot to Swindon
Ealing to Slough
Exeter to Newton Abbot
Newton Abbot to Plymouth
Newbury to Westbury
Oxford to Moreton-in-Marsh
Paddington to Ealing
Paddington to Princes Risborough
Plymouth to St. Austell
Princes Risborough to Banbury
Reading to Didcot
Slough to Newbury
St. Austell to Penzance
Swindon to Bristol
Taunton to Exeter
Westbury to Taunton

MIDLAND MAIN LINES
St. Albans to Bedford

Euston to Harrow & Wealdstone
Harrow to Watford
St. Pancras to St. Albans

COUNTRY RAILWAY ROUTES
Abergavenny to Merthyr
Andover to Southampton
Bath to Evercreech Junction
Bath Green Park to Bristol
Bournemouth to Evercreech Junction
Burnham to Evercreech Junction
Cheltenham to Andover
Croydon to East Grinstead
Didcot to Winchester
East Kent Light Railway
Fareham to Salisbury
Frome to Bristol
Guildford to Redhill
Reading to Basingstoke
Reading to Guildford
Redhill to Ashford
Salisbury to Westbury
Stratford upon Avon to Cheltenham
Strood to Paddock Wood
Taunton to Barnstaple
Wenford Bridge to Fowey
Westbury to Bath
Woking to Alton
Yeovil to Dorchester

GREAT RAILWAY ERAS
Ashford from Steam to Eurostar
Clapham Junction 50 years of change
Festiniog in the Fifties
Festiniog in the Sixties
Festiniog 50 years of enterprise
Isle of Wight Lines 50 years of change
Railways to Victory 1944-46
Return to Blaenau 1970-82
SECR Centenary album
Talyllyn 50 years of change
Wareham to Swanage 50 years of change
Yeovil 50 years of change

LONDON SUBURBAN RAILWAYS
Caterham and Tattenham Corner
Charing Cross to Dartford
Clapham Jn. to Beckenham Jn.
Crystal Palace (HL) & Catford Loop
East London Line
Finsbury Park to Alexandra Palace
Holbourn Viaduct to Lewisham
Kingston and Hounslow Loops
Lewisham to Dartford
Lines around Wimbledon
Liverpool Street to Chingford
London Bridge to Addiscombe
Mitcham Junction Lines
North London Line
South London Line
West Croydon to Epsom
West London Line
Willesden Junction to Richmond
Wimbledon to Beckenham
Wimbledon to Epsom

STEAMING THROUGH
Steaming through Cornwall
Steaming through the Isle of Wight
Steaming through Kent
Steaming through West Hants

TRAMWAY CLASSICS
Aldgate & Stepney Tramways
Barnet & Finchley Tramways
Bath Tramways
Brighton's Tramways
Bristol's Tramways
Burton & Ashby Tramways
Camberwell & W.Norwood Tramways
Clapham & Streatham Tramways
Croydon's Tramways
Dover's Tramways
East Ham & West Ham Tramways
Edgware and Willesden Tramways
Eltham & Woolwich Tramways
Embankment & Waterloo Tramways
Exeter & Taunton Tramways
Fulwell - Home to Trams, Trolleys and Buses
Great Yarmouth Tramways
Greenwich & Dartford Tramways
Hammersmith & Hounslow Tramways
Hampstead & Highgate Tramways
Hastings Tramways
Holborn & Finsbury Tramways
Ilford & Barking Tramways
Kingston & Wimbledon Tramways
Lewisham & Catford Tramways
Liverpool Tramways 1. Eastern Routes
Liverpool Tramways 2. Southern Routes
Liverpool Tramways 3. Northern Routes
Maidstone & Chatham Tramways
Margate to Ramsgate
North Kent Tramways
Norwich Tramways
Reading Tramways
Seaton & Eastbourne Tramways
Shepherds Bush & Uxbridge Tramways
Southend-on-sea Tramways
South London Line Tramways 1903-33
Southwark & Deptford Tramways
Stamford Hill Tramways
Twickenham & Kingston Tramways
Victoria & Lambeth Tramways
Waltham Cross & Edmonton Tramways
Walthamstow & Leyton Tramways
Wandsworth & Battersea Tramways

TROLLEYBUS CLASSICS
Croydon Trolleybuses
Derby Trolleybuses
Hastings Trolleybuses
Huddersfield Trolleybuses
Maidstone Trolleybuses
Portsmouth Trolleybuses
Reading Trolleybuses
Woolwich & Dartford Trolleybuses

WATERWAY ALBUMS
Kent and East Sussex Waterways
London to Portsmouth Waterway
West Sussex Waterways

MILITARY BOOKS
Battle over Portsmouth
Battle over Sussex 1940
Blitz over Sussex 1941-42
Bombers over Sussex 1943-45
Bognor at War
Military Defence of West Sussex
Military Signals from the South Coast
Secret Sussex Resistance
Surrey Home Guard

OTHER RAILWAY BOOKS
Index to all Middleton Press stations
Industrial Railways of the South-East
South Eastern & Chatham Railways
London Chatham & Dover Railway
London Termini - Past and Proposed
War on the Line (SR 1939-45)